The Master Letters of
Emily Dickinson

The Master Letters of Emily Dickinson

EDITED BY R. W. Franklin

AMHERST COLLEGE PRESS

Amherst, Massachusetts   1986

Emily Dickinson texts courtesy of Harvard University Press. Copyright ©
1958, 1986 by The President and Fellows of Harvard College.

Editorial matter and facsimiles: Copyright © 1986 by The Trustees of
Amherst College.

Publication of this work was made possible by the May H. and Albert M.
Morris '13 Fund.

Library of Congress Cataloguing in Publication Data

   Dickinson, Emily, 1830–1886.
     The Master letters of Emily Dickinson.

     Bibliography: p.
     1. Dickinson, Emily, 1830–1886—Correspondence.
   2. Poets, American—19th century—Correspondence.
   I. Franklin, R. W. (Ralph William), 1937–
   II. Title.
   PS1541.Z5A4   1986   811'.4 [B]   86–1093
    ISBN 0–943184–00–2
    ISBN 0–943184–01–0 (pbk.)

98229

Printed in the United States of America by Meriden-Stinehour Press.

INTRODUCTION

THESE THREE LETTERS, which Emily Dickinson drafted to a man she called "Master," stand near the heart of her mystery. Although there is no evidence the letters were ever posted (none of the surviving documents would have been in suitable condition), they indicate a long relationship, geographically apart, in which correspondence would have been the primary means of communication. Dickinson did not write letters as a fictional genre, and these were surely part of a much larger correspondence yet unknown to us. In the earliest one, written when both she and the Master were ill, she is responding to his initiative after a considerable silence. The tone, a little distant but respectful and gracious, claims few prerogatives from their experience, nothing more than the license to be concerned about his health, as she is about the health of all whom she loves, and to say that hearing from him again "seemed quite sweet, and wonderful." The other two letters, written a few years later, stand in impassioned contrast to this. One comes after a revelation in which she had "offend[ed] it" by telling "it the truth"; the other responds to his apparent lack of belief in what she has been professing: "One drop more from the gash that stains your Daisy's bosom – then would you *believe*?" In both she defends herself, reviewing their history, asserting her fidelity. She asks what he would do if she came "in white." She pleads to see him.

Of primary importance, the Master letters nevertheless have had an uncertain history of discovery, publication, dating, and transcription. This publication, issued at the centennial of Emily Dickinson's death, presents the three letters in chronological order, based upon new dating of the manuscripts, and provides their texts in facsimile as well as in transcriptions that show stages in the composition of each letter.

One hundred years ago, in the week following Dickinson's death on May 15, 1886, Lavinia Dickinson found what she described as a locked box containing seven hundred of her sister's poems. The Master letters may have been among them, for they were clearly not with the correspondence, which Lavinia destroyed upon discovery. It is uncertain, however, how many groups of manuscripts were found. Years later, in the midst of controversy, Lavinia maintained that there had been just one group, described now as having been in two drawers but found at one time, presumably containing not seven hundred but nearly eighteen hundred poems. Mabel Loomis Todd, who edited three volumes of the poems from the batches of manuscripts she received from Lavinia and whose notions about their discovery came from her, thought that several groups had been found. If so, the Master letters, and drafts of a few other letters that have similarly survived, may have been in one of the succeeding discoveries, if not in the first one. Lavinia, on the other hand, had parcelled out the manuscripts to both her brother's wife and his mistress and may have found it necessary to slant the truth as she told it.

By the early 1890s Mabel Todd knew of the Master letters and included a snippet—six brief sentences—in the edition of Dickinson's letters she brought out in 1894. There was no mention of "Master." The identity of the intended recipient had been concealed under the heading "*To* —— ——," and a deliberately misleading date of 1885, almost at the end of Emily Dickinson's life, had been assigned. In her 1931 revision of the 1894 *Letters* Mabel Todd, although in possession of the manuscripts, remained unwilling to print any more of the one letter, or any of the other two. She did add a note to the printed passage indicating that the manuscript was in the handwriting of the 1860s. There it stood until 1955, when Millicent Todd Bingham, who had received the manuscripts from her mother, published them for the first time in full in *Emily Dickinson's Home*. All biographical and critical studies before that date were without knowledge of their existence, text, or apparent recipient.

With the publication of *Home* in 1955, and the appearance of Thomas H. Johnson's edition of the letters three years later, and of Jay Leyda's *The Years and Hours of Emily Dickinson* two years after that, the Master letters became widely available. Millicent Bingham, puzzled by the dating of these drafts, printed them in a sequence without dates, except for one in the caption to a facsimile of the letter that begins "If you saw a bullet hit a Bird." This letter, the first in her sequence, she indicated to be "about 1861." For the others—identified here by their openings—she provided only an order: "Oh! did I offend it" followed by "I am ill, but grieving more that you are ill." The transcriptions were regularized at times in matters of punctuation, capitalization, and paragraphing. The use of pencil and ink was incompletely described. And, despite symbols for cancellations and for alternative readings, the distinction between them was blurred—especially when both conditions applied to one reading and when, among multiple readings, some had been cancelled. In the resulting text Emily Dickinson's acts of composition and revision were obscured.

While also somewhat unsure about the dating, Thomas Johnson revised Bingham's order for the letters, putting her last first, and supplied dates for all three: *about 1858* ("I am ill"), *about 1861* ("If you saw a bullet"), and *early 1862?* ("Oh, did I offend it")—numbers 187, 233, and 248 respectively in his 1958 edition. The transcriptions, based on Bingham's, though more literal and accurate than hers, had been checked against the manuscripts. But the Johnson text, employing the same symbols as Bingham's, with not much more description, also left the compositional stages obscured. Both editors omitted some inscriptions and cancellations.

Jay Leyda arranged the letters in the same order as Johnson did, but he assigned different dates, albeit with some, if more precise, uncertainty: *early spring 1858* ("I am ill"), *January? 1861* ("If you saw a bullet"), and *February? 1861* ("Oh! did I offend it"). The Leyda text is substantially different from either Bingham's or Johnson's, although it largely derived from hers and was checked, as was Johnson's, against the manuscripts. Out of the multiplicity of readings, Leyda redacted a single version. When competing readings stood uncancelled, he retained only one, choosing editorially between earlier and later ones. When competing readings did involve cancellation, he sometimes took the uncancelled reading, sometimes the cancelled one. When there was a cancelled reading with no alternatives, he often retained it, as though not to lose it entirely, but he also eliminated several such readings. Leyda was preparing copy for a compendium, not for a textual edition, and his text may be appropriate to its purpose. It is, however, a mixed version, neither initial nor final, nor indeed reflective of any particular point in the process of composition and revision.

There it has stood. The chronology in the present publication grows out of work in progress that involves dating Dickinson manuscripts anew. The effect for the Master letters is a revised order that confirms some previous dates while changing others. The letters are arranged here in the following order:

> Letter 1 *spring 1858* ("I am ill")
> Letter 2 *early 1861* ("Oh – did I offend it")
> Letter 3 *summer 1861* ("If you saw a bullet")

The sequence has been determined from aspects of Dickinson's handwriting, as the word *the*, an important example, will illustrate. Early in this period, almost without exception, Dickinson's form for *the* (lower case) consisted of two parts, a *t* separate from a linked *he*, but in 1861 she shifted to a form in which all three letters were linked.

The linked form is unknown before 1861. The earlier form appears occasionally thereafter, but the later one dominates, often accounting for more than ninety per cent of the instances. This is the pattern of the Master letters. In the first one the word *the* is always unlinked between the *t* and the *he* (13 instances). In the second letter, at a point of transition, the forms are mixed and nearly balanced in number (6 unlinked, 8 linked). In the third letter the newer form is overwhelmingly dominant (42 linked, 4 unlinked).

The first letter can be assigned to 1858, as both Johnson and Leyda thought, because of several characteristic details, one of the most distinctive being the form of *and* in which the ascender of the *d* rises strongly to the right.

This form dies out soon thereafter. Sets of quotation marks that slant downward to the left, a capital *H* made with three separate strokes, and the word *you* in a linked form—characteristics identifying early 1858—also appear.

The letter can be assigned to spring by its contents: "The Violets are by my side – the Robin very near – and 'Spring' – they say, Who is she – going by the door –"

The other two letters belong to 1861, as all previous editors have thought about the second one and Leyda about both, though in a different order. Neither letter can have been written later than the summer of 1861, since the second of them asks "Could you come to New England – this summer." It is possible that Dickinson wrote this before summer, referring to a season ahead, but the fervor of the passage as first written and her cancellation of "this summer"—perhaps as being too immediate and importunate—suggest that she was referring to the season at hand.

> I want to see you more – Sir –
> than all I wish for in
> this world – and the wish –
> altered a little – will be my
> only one – for the skies –
> Could you come to New England –
> this summer – could you come
> to Amherst – Would you like
> to come – Master?

The other letter precedes this one somewhat, but cannot with assurance be placed more precisely than "early 1861."

With the assistance of facsimile reproductions on facing pages, the line for line transcriptions seek to render the manuscripts as completely and literally as possible. Dickinson did not indent paragraphs, except for the one immediately after the salutation, and did not space between them. The beginning of a new paragraph can often be identified by space remaining on the last line of the preceding one, as can be seen at the bottom of the first page of Letter 1. Any physical line, however, that begins with a new sentence could also begin a new paragraph, and if the writing on the preceding line continues nearly to the end, it may be difficult to determine if a break were intended. In these transcriptions the most likely paragraph breaks, based on space and content, have been identified with a • to the left of the line.

Two common textual symbols, themselves not found in these manuscripts, enclose readings:

⟨ ⟩   cancelled readings

↑ ↓   inserted readings, usually above or below
        the main line of inscription

Inserted readings, identified by the arrows, are brought into the line at the related place without indication of their actual position. When specific position is important, as it often is, the facsimiles may be consulted. In turn, the transcribed text will be found to contain readings difficult to decipher in the reproductions. An appendix lists the substantive variants, including the record of cancellation, between these transcriptions and the previous ones by Bingham, Johnson, and Leyda.

Type is linear, regular, and uniform, while handwriting, Dickinson's in particular, often is not. In these manuscripts the sizes and shapes of letters will vary. Such variation has not been recorded beyond the distinction afforded by ordinary upper and lower case letters. Standard typesetting conventions have also been followed in regard to spacing and punctuation. No attempt has been made to indicate the amount of space between words, or between words and punctuation, or to indicate, for example, the length of a dash, its angle, spatial relation to adjoining words, or distance from the line of inscription. Dashes of any length are represented by an en dash, spaced on each side. Periods, commas, question marks, ending quotation marks, and the like, have no space preceding them, however situated in the manuscripts. Stray marks have been ignored. The facsimile reproductions will be helpful in all these regards. While Emily Dickinson understood italics, referring to the concept in several poems and letters, the words underlined in these manuscripts are underlined in the transcriptions as well. Italics have been used only for editorial explanation. In the notes to the transcriptions the word *over* indicates that one reading has been superimposed upon another, occupying the same space.

The manuscripts of the Master letters are now in the Emily Dickinson Collection of the Amherst College Library, numbers 827–29.

The following works, listed in chronological order, have been cited here:

Letters of Emily Dickinson, ed. Mabel Loomis Todd. 2 vols. Boston: Roberts Brothers, 1894.

Letters of Emily Dickinson, ed. Mabel Loomis Todd. New York: Harper, 1931.

Millicent Todd Bingham. *Emily Dickinson's Home: Letters of Edward Dickinson and His Family*. New York: Harper, 1955.

The Letters of Emily Dickinson, ed. Thomas H. Johnson. 3 vols. Cambridge: The Belknap Press of Harvard University Press, 1958.

Jay Leyda. *The Years and Hours of Emily Dickinson*. 2 vols. New Haven: Yale University Press, 1960.

Letter 1

Spring 1858

Manuscript: A 827. Composed of two leaves 187 x 123 mm., this sheet of stationery is wove, cream, blue-ruled, and not embossed. It has been folded, horizontally and vertically, into quarters.

Emily Dickinson set out to prepare a finished draft suitable for mailing. She wrote in ink, on letter paper, and in a deliberate, public hand. On the second page, she miswrote "indeed" as "inded" but neatly added a second "e" and continued. A drop of ink mars the top of the third page, but it may have come after she had written an awkward predication further down on the same page:

> Each Sabbath on the
> sea, makes me count
> the Sabbaths, till we
> meet on shore – and
> whether the hills will
> look as blue as the
> sailors say –

This would require obtrusive correction, and what was to have been a final draft became an intermediate one. In ink she added a potential revision here, without completing it; in ink she also revised the next sentence, cancelling several readings. If the letter were sent, another copy was made.

Dear Master
          I am ill –
but grieving more
that you are ill, I
make my stronger hand
work long eno' to tell
you – I thought perhaps
you were in Heaven,
and when you spoke
again, it seemed
quite sweet, and
wonderful, and surprised
me so – I wish that
you were well.
• I would that all I

Dear Master
            I am ill.
but - growing more
that you are ill,
make my stronger hand
work long time to tell
you. I thought perhaps
you were in Heaven,
And when you spoke
again, it seemed
quite vivid - and
wonderful, and surprised
me so - I wish that
you were well.

I would that all

love, should be weak no
more. The Pistols are
of my side. the taken
very near. and "Coming"
they say, Who is She
going by the door.
Indeed it is God's house,
And there are gates
of Heaven, and to
and fro, the Angels
go, with their sweet
postillions — I wish that
I were great. like Mr
Michael Angelo, and
could Paint for you.
You asked me what
my flowers said —
then they were
disobedient — I gave
them message.

love, should be weak no
more. The Violets are
by my side – the Robin
very near – and "Spring" –
they say, Who is she –
going by the door –
• Indeed it is God's house –
and these are gates
of Heaven, and to
and fro, the angels
go, with their sweet
postillions – I wish that
I were great, like Mr –
Michael Angelo, and
could paint for you.
• You ask me what
my flowers said –
then they were
disobedient – I gave
them messages –

7 Indeed] Inded *with a second* e *added in ink*

- They said what the
  lips in the West, say,
  when the sun goes
  down, and so says
  the Dawn –
- Listen again, Master –
- I did not tell you that
  today had been the
  Sabbath Day.
- Each Sabbath on the
  sea, makes me count
  the Sabbaths, till we
  meet on shore – ↑will the↓ and
  whether the hills will
  look as blue as the
  sailors say –
- I cannot ⟨talk⟩ ↑stay↓ any ⟨more⟩ ↑longer↓
  tonight ↑⟨now⟩↓, for this pain
  denies me –
- How strong when weak
  to recollect, and easy
  quite, to love. Will you

17–18 I cannot . . . tonight ↑⟨now⟩↓]
        successively (*a*) I cannot talk any more
                tonight
           (*b*) I cannot stay any longer
                tonight now
           (*c*) I cannot stay any longer
                tonight

They said what the
lips in the West say,
when the sun goes
down, and so says
the dawn.

Listen again, Master.
I did not tell you that
today had been the
Sabbath Sea.

Each Sabbath on the
sea, makes me count
the Sabbaths, till we
meet on Shore. And
whether the hills will
look as tall as the
endless sea. Stay longer
I cannot any more
tonight, for this pain
denies me.

How strong when weak
to recollect, and easy
quite, to love. Give you

with you, please to tell
you. soon as you are
well.

tell me, please to tell
me, soon as you are
well –

Letter 2

Early 1861

Manuscript: A 829. Composed of two leaves 187 x 123 mm., this sheet of stationery is wove, cream, gilt-edged, lightly ruled, and embossed FINE | NOTE | PAPER within a decorated vertical oval (13 x 11 mm.) The manuscript has been folded horizontally into halves.

This preliminary draft begins without a salutation and is entirely in pencil. As Dickinson wrote she also revised—cancelling words, substituting others, and setting down unresolved alternatives as she proceeded. She appears to have gone through the draft a second time, with a sharpened pencil, making further revisions but leaving many aspects unresolved. If another copy were made for mailing, many readings were determined then.

Oh – did I offend it –
⟨Did'nt it want me
to tell it the truth⟩↑‚↓
Daisy – Daisy – offend it – who
bends her smaller life to
his ↑it's↓↑‚↓ meeker ↑lower↓ every day –
who only asks – a task –
⟨who⟩ something to do for
love of it – some little way
she cannot guess to make
that master glad –
• A love so big it scares
her, rushing among her small
heart – pushing aside the
blood – and leaving her
↑all↓ faint and white in the
gust's arm –
• Daisy – who never flinched
thro' that awful parting –
but held her life so tight
he should not see the
wound – who would have
sheltered him in her
childish bosom ↑Heart↓ – only it was'nt
big eno for a Guest so large –

16 ↑all↓] *possibly an alternative for* faint and *or for* and

Oh! said I offend it —
~~Did'nt~~ ~~it want me~~
~~to tell it the truth~~
Daisy — Daisy — offend it — who
knows, her smaller life to
his [its] meeker ~~lower~~ ~~every~~ Day —
who only asks — a task —
~~who~~ Something to do for
love of it — some little way
she can not guess to make
~~that~~ master glad —
~~a~~ love so big it scares
her, rushing among her small
heart — pushing aside the
blood and [ate] aquiring her
faint and white in the
guests' arm —
Daisy — who never flinched
thro' that awful parting,
but held her life so tight
he should not see the
wound — who would have
sheltered him in her
childish [Heart] bosom — only it was'nt
big 'nos for a Guest so large —

this Louis' . guires her .
lord - and get-shirt after
slandering. perhaps she .
guired his tacts - perhaps
her odd. Boals words man
his own small
Louis' for knows all that -
but must she go un-
pardoned - teach her grow-
eiteth her majesty -
patroian things -
even the wren spoil her
nest. more than
Louis' doers -

her at the knee they tore
her over and out -
Louis' knows
a culprit - all her
her faults - master,
if it is so small
eno' to cancel with
her sins, is satisfied -
out punish - do not panish
her - shut her in prison
Sir - ony pledge that you
will prgive - some time -

- <u>This</u> Daisy – grieve her
  Lord – and yet it ↑she↓ often
  blundered – perhaps she
  grieved ↑grazed↓ his taste – perhaps
  her odd – Backwoodsman
  ⟨life⟩ ↑ways↓ ⟨troubled⟩ ↑teased↓ his finer sense ↑nature↓ –
  Daisy ⟨bea⟩ knows all that –
  but must she go un-
  pardoned – teach her grace – ↑preceptor↓
  teach her majesty –
  Slow ↑Dull↓ at patrician things –
  Even the wren opon her
  nest learns ↑knows↓ more than
  Daisy dares –
- Low at the knee that bore
  her once unto ⟨royal⟩ ↑wordless↓ rest,
  ⟨now – she⟩Daisy ⟨stoops a⟩ kneels,
  a culprit – tell her
  her ⟨offence –⟩fault – Master –
  if it is ⟨not so⟩ small
  eno to cancel with
  <u>her life</u>, ⟨Daisy⟩she is satisfied –
  but punish – do⟨ not⟩nt banish
  her – Shut her in prison –
  Sir – only pledge that you
  will forgive – sometime –

6 ⟨life⟩ . . . sense]
    successively (*a*) life troubled his finer sense
                (*b*) ways teased his finer sense
7 bea] *possibly* fea
9 ↑preceptor↓] *possibly an alternative for* grace
12 wren] *written again above the line for clarity, probably by Millicent*
    Todd Bingham
14 dares] *the s firmed up and the full word written above the line for clarity,*
    probably by Millicent Todd Bingham
17 Daisy] *over* she
19 fault] *over* –
22 she] *over* Daisy
23 do⟨ not⟩nt] nt *over* not
    successively (*a*) do not
                (*b*) dont

before the grave, and
Daisy will not mind –
she will awake in ⟨his⟩your
likeness –
• Wonder stings me more
than the Bee – who did
never sting me – but
made gay music ⟨ ⟩with
his might wherever
I ⟨may⟩ ⟨should⟩ did go –
Wonder wastes my pound,
you said I had no
size to spare –
• ⟨H⟩You send the water
over the Dam in my
brown eyes –
• I've got a cough as
big as a thimble – but
I dont care for that –
I've got a Tomahawk
in my side but that
dont hurt me ⟨h ⟩much,
⟨If you⟩ Her Master
stabs her more –
• Wont he come to her –
or will he let her ⟨ ⟩seek him,

3 your] *over* his
8 with] *over illegible word, possibly* for
14 You] *over* H
22 much] *over illegible text beginning with* h
26 seek] *over illegible letter, possibly* g

upon the grass, and
Daisy, will not mind...
she will awake in Miss
Akeness.

Women clings me more
than the Bee - who did
never cling me - but
made gay music with
his might whenever
I ~~may~~ should did go.
Women washed my pound,
you said I had no
time to spare -
She lend the water
over the Leam in no
own Eyes -
I've got a cough as
big as a thimble - but
I dont care for ~~that~~.
I've got a tomahawk
in my side but that
dont hurt me much,
~~If you~~ Her master
stabs her more -
Wont he come to her -
or will he let her seek him

never minding whatever
So long wandering home
to him at last.
Oh how the sailor strains,
when his boat is
filling — Oh how the
dying lung, till the angel
comes. Master — open
your eyes wide, and
take one in once,
I will never be tired.
I will never be noisy,
when you want to be
still. I will be ~glad~
~as the~ your best little
girl — nobody else will
see me — but you — but
that is enough — I
shall not want any
more — and all that
~heaven~ will ~hurt~
~disappoint~ me — will be
it's not so dear

never minding ⟨whateve⟩
so long wandering↑, if↓ ⟨out⟩
to him at last –
- Oh how the sailor strains,
when his boat is
filling – Oh how the
dying tug, till the angel
comes. Master – open
your life wide, and
take ⟨in⟩me in forever,
I will never be tired –
I will never be noisy
when you want to be
still – I will be ⟨glad
as the⟩ your best little
girl – nobody else will
see me, but you – but
that is enough – I
shall not want any
more – and all that
Heaven will ⟨prove⟩
↑only↓ disappoint me – ↑because↓ will be
it's not so dear

1–3 never . . . last –]
       successively (*a*) never minding whateve
                (*b*) never minding
                so long wandering out
                (*c*) never minding
                so long wandering, if
                to him at last –
10 me] *over* in
21–23 Heaven . . . dear]
       successively (*a*) Heaven will prove
                (*b*) Heaven will
                disappoint me – will be
                it's not so dear
                (*c*) Heaven will
                only disappoint me – because will be
                it's not so dear
22 ↑because↓] *possibly an alternative for* will be

Letter 3

Summer 1861

Manuscript: A 828. Two sheets of stationery, each comprising two leaves 202 x 127 mm. The paper is laid, cream with a blue rule, and embossed with a decorative frame (13 x 11 mm.) containing a queen's head above the letter L. The manuscript has been folded horizontally into thirds.

Written in ink, revised in ink and pencil, this letter was begun as a final draft suitable for sending. On the first page Dickinson neatly reworked "He" into "I dont" so that the change was inconspicuous, and on the third page, for clarity, she touched up the "e" in "breast." Although she continued on, the draft became intermediate on the fourth page. There, near the top, in ink, she cancelled the word "our"; further down, knowing that this would now not be a final copy, she wrote the alternative wording "remember that" above the line, also in ink. All the other revisions were in pencil, made after she had finished with pen. She went back through the whole letter, making many changes, and added two passages at the end, one marked for insertion in the midst of a change on the second page, the other unmarked.

Master.

    If you saw a bullet
hit a Bird – and he told you
he was'nt shot – you might weep
at his courtesy, but you would
certainly doubt his word –
- One drop more from the gash
that stains your Daisy's
bosom – then would you <u>believe</u>?
Thomas' faith in anatomy – was
stronger than his faith in faith.
God made me – ⟨Sir⟩ – ↑Master –↓ I did'nt
be – myself – ⟨He⟩<u>I</u> dont know how
it was done – He built the
heart in me – Bye and bye
it outgrew me – and like
the little mother – with the
big child – I got tired
holding him – I heard of a
thing called "Redemption" – which
rested men and women –

13 <u>I</u> dont] *in ink over* He *with part of* H *reworked into* <u>I</u>

Master.

If you saw a bullet
hit a Bird - and he told you
he wasn't shot - you might weep
at his courtesy, but you would
certainly doubt his word -
One drop more from the gash
that stains your Daisy's
bosom - then would you believe?
Thomas' faith in Anatomy, was
stronger than his faith in faith.
God made me - [Master -] I didn't
be - myself. [I don't] know how
it was done. He built the
heart in me - Bye and bye
it outgrew me - and like
the little mother - with the
big child - I got tired
holding him - I heard of a
thing called "Redemption" - which
rested men and women -

You remember I asked you
for it – you gave me something
else. I forgot the Redemption
~~in the~~ ~~Redeemed~~ – ~~I did n't~~
~~tell you for a long time but~~
~~I knew you had altered me~~ –
~~I~~ and ~~was tired~~ – no more – ~~(so) Roar~~
~~did (this) stranger (Become that~~
~~was if, or my breath – the~~
~~Alternative – I had tossed~~
~~the fellow away with the smile)~~.
I am older – tonight, Master –
but the love is the same.
So are the moon and the
Crescent – If it had been
God's will that I might
breathe where you breathed –
And find the place – myself –
At night – if I ~~never~~ forget,
that I am not with you –
And that sorrow and frost –
are nearer than I – if I wish

You remember I asked you
for it – you gave me something
else – I forgot the Redemption
⟨in the Redeemed – I did'nt
tell you for a long time – but
I knew you had altered me –
I⟩ ↑and↓ was tired – no more ↑+↓ ⟨– so dear
did this stranger become, that
were it, or my breath – the
alternative – I had tossed
the fellow away with a smile.⟩
• I am older – tonight, Master –
but the love is the same –
so are the moon and the
crescent – If it had been
God's will that I might
breathe where you breathed –
and find the place – myself –
at night – if I ↑can↓ never forget
that I am not with you –
and that sorrow and frost
are nearer than I – if I wish

7 more ↑+↓] *the text keyed for insertion is at the end of the letter*

with a might I cannot
repress – that mine were the
Queen's place – the love of
the – Plantagenet is my only
apology – To come nearer
than Presbyteries – and nearer than
the new coat – that the Tailor
made – the prank of the Heart
at play on the Heart – in holy
Holiday – is forbidden me –

- You make me say it over –
- I fear you laugh – when I do
not see – ⟨but⟩ "Chillon" is not
funny. Have you the Heart in
your breast – Sir – is it set
like mine – a little to the left –
has it the misgiving – if it
wake in the night – perchance –
itself to it – a timbrel is it –
itself to it a tune?
- These things are ⟨reverent⟩ ↑holy↓, Sir,
I touch them ⟨reverently⟩ ↑hallowed↓, but

15 breast] *the* e *reworked in ink for clarity*

with a might I cannot
express – that mine nor the
Queen's place – the Tomb of
the Plantagenet – is my one
apology – to come nearer
than Presbyters – and nearer than
the new Coat – that the Tailor
made – the prank of the Heart
At play on the Heart – in holy
Holiday – is forbidden me –
Then make me say it over –
I hear you laugh – when I do
not be – ~~####~~ "Chillon" is not
funny – Have you the Heart – in
your Breast – Sir – is it set
like mine – a little to the left –
has it the Misgiving – if it
wake in the night – perchance –
itself to it – a timbrel is it –
itself to it a tune?
these things are ~~innocent~~ Sir,
I touch them ~~####~~ , but –

persons who pray — Can demark
"Father"! You say I do
not tell you all — "Daisy" confessed
and denied not —
Vesuvius dont talk — Etna dont —
said a syllable — one of them —
a thousand years ago, and
Pompeii heard it — and hid
forever — She could'nt look the
world in the face, afterward —
I suppose — Bashful Pompeii!
"Tell you of the want" — you
know what a leech is, dont
you — and Daisy's arm is small —
And you have felt the horizon
hav'nt you — and did the
sea — never come so close as
to make you dance?
I dont know what you can
do for it — thank you — Master —

persons who pray – dare remark
⟨our⟩ "Father!" You say I do
not tell you all – Daisy "confessed –
and denied not."
- Vesuvius dont talk – Etna – dont –
⟨They⟩ ↑2↓ said a syllable – ↑1↓ one of them –
a thousand years ago, and
Pompeii heard it, and hid
forever – She could'nt look the
world in the face, afterward –
I suppose – Bashful Pompeii!
- "Tell you of the want" – you
know what a leech is, dont
you – and ↑⟨remember that⟩↓ Daisy's arm is small –
and you have felt the Horizon –
hav'nt you – and did the
sea – ↑n↓ever come so close as
to make you dance?
- I dont know what you can
do for it – thank you – Master –

2 our] *cancelled in ink*
6 ⟨They⟩ . . . them –]
       successively (*a*) They said a syllable – one of them –
                (*b*) one of them – said a syllable –
14 remember that] *written in ink, cancelled in pencil*
17 ↑n↓ever] ever *written in ink;* n *added in pencil*

– but if I had the Beard on
my cheek – ↑like you –↓ and you – had Daisy's
petals – and you cared so for
me – what would become of you?
Could you forget ↑me↓ in fight, or
flight – or the foreign land?
• Could'nt Carlo, and you and I
walk in the meadows an hour –
and nobody care but the Bobolink –
and <u>his</u> – a <u>silver</u> scruple?
I used to think when I died –
I could see you – so I died
as fast as I could – but the
"Corporation" are going ↑too↓ – so ⟨Eternity⟩ ↑Heaven↓
wont be sequestered – ⟨at all⟩ ↑now↓ –
• Say I may wait for you –
• Say I need go with no stranger
to the to me – untried ⟨country⟩ ↑fold↓ –
I waited a long time – Master –
but I can wait more – wait
till my hazel hair is dappled –

14–15 "Corporation" . . . ↑now↓ –]
      successively (*a*) "Corporation" are going – so Eternity
               wont be sequestered – at all –
           (*b*) "Corporation" are going too – so Heaven
               wont be sequestered – now –

- but if I had the Beard on
my Cheek - and you like you, you -had Cairo's
Kilits - and you Cared so for
me - what - would become of you?
Could you forget me in fight, or
flight - or the foreign land?
Could'nt Carlo - and you and I
walk in the meadows an hour -
And nobody Care but the Bobolink -
And his - A Silver scruple?
I used to think when I died -
I could see you - so I died
as fast as I could - but the
"Corporation" are going too so Heaven
wont be Sequestered - now All -
Say I may wait for you -
Say I need go with no Stranger
to the to me - untried fold Country -
I waited a long time - Master -
but I can wait more - wait
till my hazel hair is dappled -

And you carry the clue —
then I can look at my
watch — And if the Day is
too far declined — we can take
the chances for Heaven —
What would you do with me
if I came in white?
Have you the little chest to
put the alive — in?
I want to see you more Sir —
than all I wish for in
this world — And the wish —
altered a little — will be my
only one — for the skies —
Could you come to New England —
would
~~this~~ ~~Summer~~ — ~~Could~~ you come
to Amherst — Would you like
to come — Master?
~~Would~~ ~~it~~ do ~~harm~~ — yet ~~so~~ ~~with~~
~~you~~ ~~Sir~~ — Could Daisy disappoint
you — no — she wouldn't — Sir —
it were comfort forever — just —

and you carry the cane –
then I can look at my
watch – and if the Day is
too far declined – we can take
the chances ⟨of⟩ ↑for↓ Heaven –
- What would you do with me
  if I came "in white"?
- Have you the little chest – to
  put the alive – in?
- I want to see you more – Sir –
  than all I wish for in
  this world – and the wish –
  altered a little – will be my
  only one – for the skies –
- Could you come to New England –
  ⟨this summer – could⟩ ↑Would↓ you come
  to Amherst – Would you like
  to come – Master?
- ⟨Would it do harm – yet we both
  fear God –⟩ Would Daisy disappoint
  you – no – she would'nt – Sir –
  it were comfort forever – just

to look in your face, while
you looked in mine – then I
could play in the woods – till
Dark – till you take me
where sundown cannot find
us – and the true keep
coming – till the town is full.
⟨Will you tell me if you will?⟩

I did'nt think to tell you, you
did'nt come to me "in white" –
nor ever told me why –

+ No Rose, yet felt myself
a'bloom,
No Bird – yet rode in Ether –

9–11 I did'nt think . . . why –] *written in pencil*
12–14 + No Rose . . . Ether –] *written in pencil; these lines of verse are keyed*
for insertion into the letter text on p. 35

to Cook in your face, while
you Cooked in mine. then I
could play in the wood till
dark - till you take me
when Sundown cannot find
us - and the trees keep
Coming - till the town is full.
~~till~~ ~~you~~ ~~the~~ ~~me~~ ~~I~~ ~~you~~ ~~will~~

I did'nt think to tell you, you
did'nt come to me "in white",
nor ever told me why,

+ No Rose, yet felt myself
a'bloom,
No Bird - yet rode in Ether.

APPENDIX

The following list of variants between the present text and three others is limited to substantives, including the record of their cancellation by Emily Dickinson. Other aspects of apparatus are not included, nor are differences in accidentals, such as punctuation, capitalization, and spelling. The symbols referring to other texts are:

B Millicent Todd Bingham. *Emily Dickinson's Home: Letters of Edward Dickinson and His Family* (New York: Harper, 1955), pp. 422–32.

J *The Letters of Emily Dickinson*, ed. Thomas H. Johnson (Cambridge: The Belknap Press of Harvard University Press, 1958), II, 333, 373–75, 391–92.

L Jay Leyda. *The Years and Hours of Emily Dickinson* (New Haven: Yale University Press, 1960), I, 352–53; II, 22–25.

Square brackets, the symbol used in *B* and *J* to indicate cancellation, appear incidentally in a few of the variants cited below. In *B* cancelled readings were also set in italics, which have not been retained here. In the following list italics have been used only for editorial explanation.

Letter 1

16.13 will the] *not present L*
16.17 talk] *not cancelled B, J, L*
16.17 stay] *not present L*
16.17 any] *repeated B, J*
16.17 more] *not cancelled B, J, L*
16.17 longer] *not present L*
16.18 now] *not cancelled B, J, L*

Letter 2

22.2–3 Did'nt . . . truth] *not cancelled L*
22.6 it's] *not present L*
22.6 lower] *not present L*
22.7 task] *taste B*
22.8 who] *not present L*
22.16 all] *not present B, L*
22.24 bosom] *not present L*
25.2 it] *not present L*
25.4 grazed] *not present L*
25.6 life] *not present L*
25.6 troubled] *not present L*
25.6 nature] *not present L*
25.7 bea] *fea B, J; not present L*
25.11 Dull] *not present L*
25.13 learns] *not present L*
25.16 unto] *with B*

25.16 royal] *not present L*
25.17 now] *not present L*
25.17 she] *not present B, J, L*
25.17 stoops a] stoops *B; not present L*
25.19 offence] *not present L*
25.20 not so] *not present L*
25.22 Daisy] *not present L*
25.23 do⟨ not⟩nt] do not [dont] *B;* [do not] dont *J;* do not *L*
26.3 his] *not present B, L*
26.8 ⟨ ⟩with] with *B, J, L*
26.10 may] *not present L*
26.10 should] *not present L*
26.14 ⟨H⟩You] You *B, J, L*
26.22 ⟨h ⟩much] much *B, J, L*
26.23 If you] *not present L*
26.26 ⟨ ⟩seek] seek *B, J, L*
29.1 whateve] whatere *B;* whatever *J; not present L*
29.2 out] *not present L*
29.10 ⟨in⟩me] me *B, J, L*
29.14-15 glad as the] *not present L*
29.20-23 and all . . . dear] and all that Heaven will be will disappoint me, only because it's not so dear *B, L;* and all that Heaven only will disappoint me – will be because it's not so dear *J*
29.21 prove] *not present B, J, L*

Letter 3

32.12 Sir] *not present L*
32.13 ⟨He⟩I dont] I dont *B, J, L*
35.4-7 in the Redeemed . . . I] *not cancelled L*
35.7 and] *not present L*
35.7-11 so dear . . . smile] *not present L*
36.13 but] *not present L*
36.21 reverent] *not present L*
36.22 reverently] *not cancelled L*
36.22 hallowed] *not present L*
39.2 our] *not cancelled L*
39.6 They] thy *B;* Thy *J; not present L*
39.6 ↑₂↓ said . . . them] *text rearranged without numbering B, J, L*
39.14 remember that] *not present L*
39.17 ↑n↓ever] never *B, J, L*
40.14-15 "Corporation" . . . now] "Corporation" are going Heaven too so [Eternity] wont be sequestered—now [at all] *B, J*
40.14 Eternity] *not present L*
40.15 at all] *not present L*
40.18 country] *not present L*
43.5 of] *not present L*
43.16 this summer] *not cancelled L*
43.16 could] *not present L*
43.19-20 Would it . . . God] *not cancelled L*
44.8 Will you . . . will?] *not present L*
44.12-14 No Rose . . . Ether] *inserted at marked place in text L*